Planet Protectors

Stories of Green Heroes

Bahar Dutt

THE ENERGY AND RESOURCES INSTITUTE
Creating Innovative Solutions for a Sustainable Future

From the Desk of Dr Vibha Dhawan

Climate change is a reality that is impacting each one of us. The environment is grappling with many adversities: pollution, endangered ecosystems and species, to rising natural disasters and climate anomalies. The year 2023 was confirmed as the warmest year in the global temperature data records since 1850. The picture is bleak indeed; yet, we must remember that even the darkest night ends and the sun rises again. With multiple challenges threatening the future of our world, it becomes imperative to act urgently and collectively.

Numerous efforts are being undertaken by governments and organizations, we must also do our bit to save our planet. However, it can be confusing, or even overwhelming, to know just how or where to begin. This book, *Planet Protectors: Stories of Green Heroes,* guides us on just that: how little steps can make a big difference. Comprising stories of ordinary individuals, like you and me, who did extraordinary things to protect and conserve the environment. These stories inspire and encourage the readers by showcasing innovative ways of making a difference at the local level: be it reviving traditional practices of architecture or farming, cleaning beaches, or turning a landfill into a park, or even saving rare animals by creating awareness. The book aims to instil responsibility amongst children towards their environment. To make the contents fun to read, the book indulges young minds' curiosity by adding magical elements to elevate comprehension.

Planet Protectors nurtures its readers to become contentious leaders of tomorrow, who will join (and hopefully succeed) in humankind's race to combat climate change. We must all play a role in this global effort at our local level. Our hope with *Planet Protectors* is to give rise to many such 'superheroes' who will save our world, through the power of motivating stories that are equally practical.

Vibha Dhawan

Director-General, TERI

For Aranya,

Thank you for taking me to the world of 'Honey Leopards, Pink Dragonflies, and Sour Lions'.

Contents

DEAR MUMMY, HOW CAN I SAVE THE WORLD?

Tucked in her bed, Aranya was frowning. "Mumma so many people are cutting trees and every time we drive out of the city I see that big mountain of garbage that makes me cough. When I grow up Mumma, I will not let this happen", she said.

"Really?", asked her Mumma. She then said, "Okay, how about we go on an adventure to explore how we can make this happen?"

And so, deep in the stillness of the night, Aranya and her sister Prakriti set off to The Land of Talking Trees to meet Taro, the wise old tree. Their mother's voice gently guided them through valleys, mountains, and fields. Thuddd!!!! And suddenly they were standing in front of Taro. They could feel Taro's octopus like gnarled branches swishing in the air.

Taro as a rule was quite grumpy, but he made an exception for young children, "Hello my kids, what brings you here today?" he asked politely.

"We want to know how we can save the world?" replied the girls stuttering and stammering, and crouching to avoid Taro's branches. Pleasantly surprised at their question, Taro lifted the two girls onto his tallest branch and said, "Come. Let's go on an adventure and I will show you the heroes who helped save my magical kingdom. In this wondrous land you will meet Sour Lions and Honey Leopards, and Pink Dragonflies too—and the people trying to save these unique creatures".

Clutching onto the backs of the Sour Lions, they soared through a bright orange sky. "Beware of the Rirartell Snakes" warned Taro, "they have big slithery bodies and are usually found in 'Youritasaus', the forest patch that's right below the Sticky Swamps".

And so began their journey. Aranya and Prakriti were going to come back with many practical ideas to save the world!

THE OLD MAN AND HIS MAGIC SEEDS

Up in the high mountains of Uttarakhand, lived an old man with the sweetest, kindest smile and a beard that reached up to his knees.

Jardhariji, as he was fondly called, was a bit of a mystery to everyone. He travelled from one village to another distributing magic seeds that he pulled out from his long grey kurta, giving him the appearance of a wizard from an ancient land.

Jardhariji would hold the seeds in his wrinkled hands and they would shine like dazzling gemstones against the bright sun. Some were black like the night sky, others ruby red like cherries, while some were dark brown like the mountain side.

He would teach the farmers how to nurture these traditional seeds, so that they did not have to buy these from the market.

In the year 2008 there was no rain. Forests all over Uttarakhand had turned brown and lush fields turned yellow as the crops dried up. But the village that had followed Jardhariji's advise was bursting with fruits and legumes.

This was the ancient method of farming that the mountain people had long forgotten. Known as 'Bara-anaj' farming, it involved multi-cropping of cereals and legumes grown at different times of the year, so the farmers had food all year long. Soon all villages across Uttarakhand, inspired by Jardhariji, started going back to the old methods of farming.

And now, it was time for Jardhariji to move to another region, his pockets jingling with seeds waiting to be sown soon.

THE TIDE TURNER

In a land by the sea, lived a giant monster with a mouth so wide,
that he could eat all the garbage and litter brought in by the tide.

One day the monster got an upset tummy,
whatever he ate made him feel crummy
Along came a lawyer who said,
"This monster, I must persuade
to eat only that which can bio-degrade."

So Afroz began to teach the people what to throw out
for it was their waste that most certainly led the monster to gout...

He worked night and day, down by the bay
gathering rubber, plastic, papers, and all that came his way.
Big trucks came laden every day,
to take the filth that the monster belched away

Afroz got tired and low
but he did not stop or go slow,
for he had made a promise to the monster
And soon enough hundreds of people also joined his endeavour

By next spring, the monster felt better,
and the Olive Ridley turtles roamed unfettered.

The beach was clean, the deal was sealed!
No longer could you find garbage by the sea.
The monster's tummy was at last fully healed!

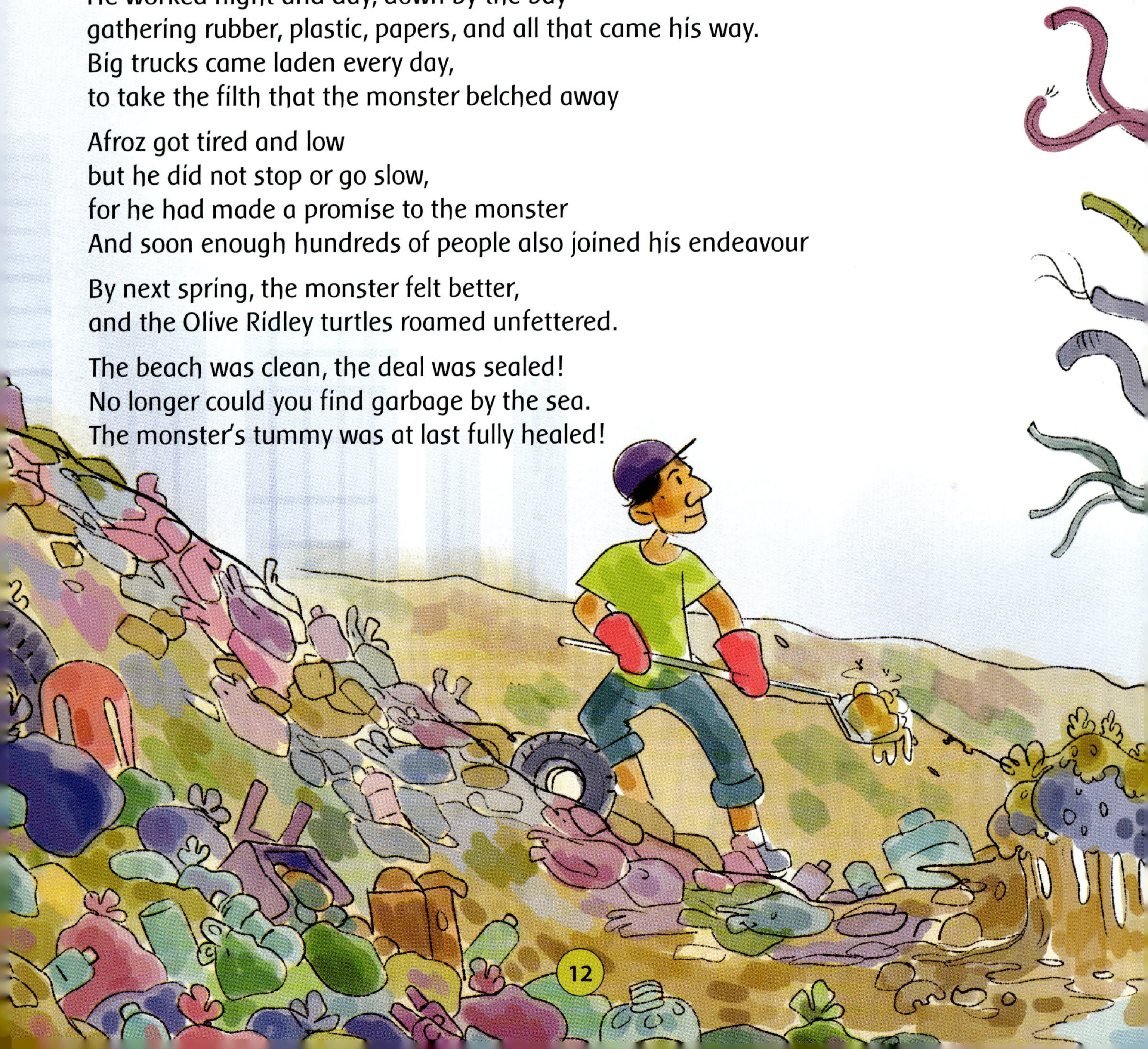

THE MAGIC POT OF BLACK GOLD

There was a lady called Compost-Waali
who taught people that throwing food away was a big folly
She made a magic pot that converts to black gold
all your food waste that would otherwise mould

But banana peels and egg shells can be vehement
in their absolute refusal to ferment
So she made a magic mix,
a part of her bag of tricks
that came free with a 'Mitti Ka Pot'
It is really the most elegant bin you could have bought

It is called the Daily Dump
they even have a helpline, in case you hit a bump
So why not start composting right in your house?
There's no fear of flies, insects, or even a mouse

Yes, it smells like 'geeli mitti'
and if you don't like that, what a pity!

Every kitchen generates food waste,
but if you compost, your emissions are erased
Now you can reduce the mountains of trash
No longer will your city burn with ash

It reduces pollution
and that's a wonderful solution!
Let us join hands with Poonam Bir Kasturi
who has helped reduce our carbon footprint, hugely

THE SCIENTIST WHO SPEAKS TO ELEPHANTS

In the sleepy little hill station of 'Tea and Biscuits', there lived a herd of elephants who munched on leaves and grass all day. You could spot their grey backs standing out against the tiny tea bushes. This town, where rain drops melted into coffee pods and monkeys looked like Sour Lions produced the best tea in the world.

The highlight of the day was the evening tea-party. Having foraged in the forest all day long, the elephants would arrive at sunset. The mothers nudged the nervous babies forward, while teenage ellies scurried down the hill, their legs not keeping pace with their heavy bodies. Balancing the biscuits gingerly on their trunks, the elephants

would dip them in lukewarm tea. The party continued till the sun rolled down the hills, making silhouettes against their backs. What a fine end to a day!

But as all parties do, sometimes they became too unruly. In their frenzy, elephants would trample on tea bushes or knock down homes, sending the hoo-mans in town into panic. Scared of troubling the hoo-mans, the Elephant Council sought scientist Ananda's advice. "How can we hold our party without disturbing our friends, the hoo-mans?"

Ananda did not fit into the regular look of a scientist. He didn't wear a white coat, or work in a laboratory. He came with a paper and a pen, and wore a hat. To help the elephants, he climbed trees and spent long hours crouching behind a tea bush, taking notes on a sheet of paper.

"The peace of the town of 'Tea and Biscuits' is getting disturbed", Ananda reprimanded the pachyderms. "You have trampled the tea bushes; the babies have even squashed some of the flowerpots, and laundry that was left out to dry is now caked in mud. They are making plans to send you away" he whispered, "but I have a plan". "I am all ears", said the matriarch leaning forward. Almost 70 years old, with her long lashes and big ears, she was the wise one. No wonder the herd had selected her as their leader.

"Why don't you alert me every evening with the location of your tea party and I will make sure no one disturbs you", volunteered Ananda. He suggested they set up a lantern that would be hoisted on the top of the hill. When it was red, it meant the elephants were camping on this side of town and hoo-mans should avoid the area.

When it was green, it was safe for the hoo-mans to move. "These hoo-mans have phones, so I can also send them a message alert", said Ananda.

And that's how the elephants in the sleepy town of 'Tea and Biscuits' continued to enjoy their daily tea party. Ananda would send an 'SMS' to all the hoo-mans in town to alert them of the elephants' festivities. Here's what the message read:

The elephants are having their tea party in Long Garden Tea Estate today. Those living close by should be careful.

He also set up a big lantern that blinked like a lighthouse on top of a hill, sending out a clear warning to the people of 'Tea and Biscuits'.

Soon, a year had gone by and not a single disaster had been reported; Ananda was delighted. "Science can often help solve complex problems", declared Ananda as he sipped tea with the matriarch.

THE PENGUIN WHO SAVED THE DAY

The Land of Talking Trees was ruled by a King whose court had two teams of advisors. Team one, the Polluter Penguins lived in big houses by the lake. While team two comprised only Fairy Penguin Nitwit. Next to the pack of Polluter Penguins, who were much taller and bigger in size, Nitwit looked too little.

One day Nitwit was munching on his lunch—sandwiches with green worms and red cheese—in his office, when he was distracted by a buzz coming from the doorway.

Upon investigating, he saw a bright pink light shining through the dark corridors. That could only mean one thing. The Honey Leopard and the Pink Dragonfly had arrived for a meeting. The creatures of the forest were in a state of panic as the Polluter Penguins were taking over the mountain That Is Home. They wanted to crush the mountain and turn it into large bricks for their state-of-the-art homes overlooking the lake. "Can you help us, please?" said the Honey Leopard meekly.

"Hmm...yes!" said Nitwit. "But for that I must don my magic black coat that will help turbocharge my brain". Wearing the magic coat, he arrived at the King's palace to complain. The Polluter Penguins were already there, cackling amongst themselves when Nitwit entered the court.

Nitwit gave them a side glance and muttered the magic spell that gave him confidence:

By the power of this black coat, and the magic of God's oath, give me the courage, Gillee gillee Gillespie,
To save nature's glory!

Let the arguments begin, gestured the King. The Polluter Penguins presented a map showing the big houses for the Lake City people. "A conveyor belt will carry them from their houses to the shopping mall, where the brain maps will download data and robots will carry their purchases to the cash registers. All offices will be connected with golf carts. As for the wild animals who lived in the forest, we will build hotels for them. They will be fed hygienic food served on trays and special air would be streamed through purifiers. It will be an 'Intelligent City' that would be controlled by our great King at the press of a button". It seemed like a grand plan indeed.

Now it was Nitwit's turn. He cleared his throat and started, "The mountain That Is Home is the source of sparkling blue water. The forests cool our land, bringing in a gentle breeze. The Honey Leopards shine so bright that they light up the dim sky. A ride on the backs of the Pink Dragonflies offers panoramic views of the mountaintop. The soil shines like black gold, reaping food unlike nowhere else. If there is magic anywhere, it is here on the mountain That Is Home! How do you put a price on all this, our dear King?"

By now, the King was in tears and the Polluter Penguins shook their heads. "No more!" said the King. "The Fairy Penguin Nitwit is right. The best things in life are free, let's keep it that way." The Polluter Penguins waddled out grunting in disgust, as the Pink Dragonflies and Honey Leopards hugged each other with relief. Nitwit had saved their home.

A WOMEN'S ARMY AND THE UGLIEST BIRD IN THE WORLD

Eight-year-old Purnima was sitting on the edge of the Brahmaputra River, her chin resting on her knees, when suddenly a mighty bird swooped down and sat in front of her. The people in her village called this bird, with a razor-sharp beak and steel grey eyes, the 'ugly' bird. But, sitting up close to it, Purnima thought this bird looked magnificent.

Young Purnima would often come to sit by the river, she did not have too many friends. Her grandmother had taught her the names of many birds in her native language Assamese. This one was called the 'Hargilla'.

Looking at the tears running down Purnima's face the wise old Hargilla said in a comforting voice, "Don't cry little girl", as it wrapped its giant wing around her to comfort her. Today she had been scolded for climbing trees in her *mekhela-chadar*, a traditional dress worn by women from Assam. A few minutes with the Hargilla and Purnima was already feeling better. From that day on, she would sit by the river chatting with the Hargilla for many hours.

One day a huge storm hit the village of Dadara, where the Hargilla birds had built their nests. The birds were in despair as the branches menacingly swayed in the wind putting the chicks in grave danger.

The chicks had not yet learned to fly and some of them just tumbled out of their nests with the gales. Purnima remembered the many hours she had spent chatting with her friend. She scrambled out of bed; she had to do something! She started by grabbing the furry chicks and wrapping them in cloth to keep them warm, while she took them to the nearby zoo. Within a few weeks, the rescued chicks were better and ready to go back to their homes.

The Hargilla bird was hated in the village due to its food habits. A scavenging bird that ate flesh and bones, the people of Dadara thought it brought bad luck wherever it went. But Purnima started by reaching out to the women, "the Hargilla is our friend, it is like nature's cleaning army. How can we hate this bird? Let's make a pact with these birds—you keep our village clean and you can nest in our trees forever", Purnima suggested at the village meeting.

The transformation was slow, but soon the women of the village were convinced. Now anytime a Hargilla male bird started making a nest, the women would celebrate by cutting a birthday cake in anticipation.

They knew a Hargilla baby was on its way! Soon the Hargilla Army passed a diktat: no one could chop the trees in the village, or cause any harm to the chicks.

Purnima taught them another skill. She trained the women to weave motifs of the Hargilla on their traditional Assamese scarves. The women of Dadara sold these scarves at a good price and soon Dadara became world famous as the village that saved the Greater Adjutant Stork. People came from all over the world to learn how this village was protecting a critically endangered bird. By now, Purnima had finished her studies and become a conservation biologist. In order to collect data on the Greater Adjutant Stork, she constructed a 20 feet high tower to observe the birds in their nests. "When I am up on the *machan* with the storks, I forget everything. It is just me and them", said Purnima fondly.

THE LEGEND OF THE MINI FOREST

It was a sweltering hot afternoon in the town of 'Pollutionabad'. Sixteen-year-old Samarrth peeped out of his window restlessly! The pollution was so high here that children could venture out only in the afternoon, when the sun was at its peak. By evening the entire town was covered in a swirl of dust and smog. It was impossible to see even the tallest buildings.

As soon as the clock struck four, Samarrth rushed out on his cycle, his head brimming with ideas. On his way back from school, he had noticed a patch of land filled with rubbish. And yet, there was something about that small piece of land that beckoned him.

What if he cleared the rubbish and let the soil hidden under years of junk breathe again? What if he and his friends got together every week and turned this into a mini forest? A forest that carried the scents of different plants, rather than

the awful stench of decomposed food. Samarrth rubbed his hands in delight. "I have been frustrated for so long because there isn't any forest near our homes, lets create one!", he told his friends in their 'Club Meeting' that evening.

And that's how the Mini Forest was created. Every afternoon, six of them would arrive at the site and start cleaning. Within a month or so, they managed to clear nearly 4000 kilos of waste and began to plant species that were once found here. Within a year the land was buzzing with life. In the day there were dazzling dragonflies who hovered above the little pond; there were climber plants that enabled the fairies and goblins to ascend to the treetops for their picnics at night, by the light of the fireflies. Birds of different colours started visiting the Mini Forest, along with butterflies with wisps of orange and yellow.

News of this Mini Forest had spread and the King invited Samarrth to create such patches all over the town. After a few years, the King had renamed the town 'Haridabad', as it was now covered in a carpet of green.

THE MUD HOME-MAKER

The day young Biju Bhaskar arrived at the School of Architecture, he felt like he had conquered the universe. However, after a few days in class, he could feel a huge grey cloud hovering over his head. He asked his teachers, "Why do we make concrete structures with straight lines, when everything in nature is found in waves or curves?"

As part of his course, Biju was studying complex equations with mathematics and physics and learning to build homes that required a lot of energy to construct. But he was clear, "I want to work with the earth's energy, not against it".

And so, he set off for the School of Nature—here there were no straight lines. The rivers ran crooked, the trees were bent like a 'C', and people built houses with walls as crooked as the wriggly worm. He called it his year of unlearning. He lived with tribals in the forest and learned how they used bamboo, grass, and mud to make their homes. He met a wise sage in Madhya Pradesh who became his 'guru'. The guru taught him when to pluck plants from the forest and how to use them for constructing homes.

In the School of Nature, not one artificial material was used. Instead, plants of all shapes, sizes, and colours were made into a magic paste.

Biju learned to weave walls with bamboo and make homes with compressed earth and natural materials. His homes were easy to make and used just half of the resources that were used by the methods of the School of Architecture.

Finally, he was back in his village in Tamil Nadu. He set up a school where students of architecture could come and 'unlearn' all the concepts that they were taught in their universities. They came to learn about the texture of different plants, their time of flowering, and how the principles of nature could be applied to the built environment. Soon, students from across India started coming to learn how to build with mud.

THE BAREFOOT ECOLOGIST

Six-year-old Aranya didn't like school. All she wanted to do was go to the nearby park and search for ladybirds. "What if they taught us how to collect bugs and fallen leaves from the ground? Or gather little twigs that I can carry in my cloth bag and make little bug homes with?", she wondered to her Nani.

"Have you heard the story of Tulsi Gowda?", her Nani asked as Aranya burrowed herself in Nani's blanket, holding her hands that smelled of cold cream. Nani continued, "She was given the Padma Shri."

"Who's that?" asked Aranya, her curiosity piqued. "Well", said Nani and began to recite a story:

Tulsi Gowda is as old as me and lives in a small village in Karnataka. One day the postman came with a letter; she had been invited by the President of India, to receive an award for planting over 30,000 trees. Tulsi Ajji, as everyone fondly called her, couldn't understand what the fuss was about. "I have spent my entire life in the forest, quietly watching when the seeds sprout in the season, but I haven't been to school" she wondered, "I don't have any fancy knowledge, why would they give me an award?"

Life had not been easy for Tulsi, who lost her husband when she was very young.

She then started accompanying her mother to a nearby nursery managed by the forest department. Officials at the department were so impressed by the way she looked after the saplings that she worked with them for over 60 years.

Ajji knew how to identify every single tree in the forest. Everyone asked, "Ajji, where did you learn about the forest?". Tulsi proudly replied, "I speak the language of nature".

"You see, you don't have to read lots of books to know more about nature", said Nani, "start where you are, like Tulsi Gowda".

SAVING THE PALAPOOVAN

In a small town in Kerala, there lived a lonely turtle named Tapoo. "I wonder what the world is like beyond my home", he mourned one humid afternoon. To remedy this, he booked himself a cruise on the Chandragiri River, but the pier was quite far from the underwater stones where he lived.

On the day of his cruise, he set out early in the morning with a suitcase strapped to his back to reach the pier on time. After a while, he met a trail of ants marching forward in a single file, who assured him that he was moving in the right direction. By mid-day the sun was beating down, so Tapoo kept dipping his body in the river to cool himself. Just as he was swimming the last mile where the cruise boat would be waiting for him, he felt some nylon ropes clamping on his back, first pulling him down underwater and then flinging him in the air! Tapoo was entangled in a fisherman's net.

Tapoo was extremely scared and slightly befuddled, when suddenly he heard a voice: "Please let him go! This is the Asian Giant Softshell turtle!"

The turtle was fondly known as the 'Palapoovan' to local fishermen.

It was the voice of a young woman who had been camping next to the river for several months now. The ropes were snapped and the kind fisherman let Tapoo slither to the middle of the river. Tapoo used the currents of the river to carry himself to where the cruise boat was waiting for him.

Upon reaching the boat he was welcomed with a hot towel and a tall glass of orange juice. He was relieved and waved and cheered, "Yoo hoo! I made it". Tapoo was waving to Ayushi, his savior who had helped him start his journey to discover the world.

A few hours later, as he sat on the deck of the boat overlooking a beautiful sunset, he was immensely pleased. Thinking of Ayushi with a smile, he said to himself, "the world indeed is a wonderful place, you just need to step out of your shell".

MEET THE REAL HEROES FROM ARANYA AND PRAKRITI'S ADVENTURES

Vijay Jardhari started the Beej Bachao Andolan (Save the Seeds Campaign) in 1986 to save traditional varieties of seeds that would otherwise have vanished. He marched across Uttarakhand to convince farmers to revive the Bara-Anaj (12 grains) system of farming. This is a traditional method of mixed farming of different species—lentils, cereals, vegetables, legumes, and creepers—grown in harmony with each other using traditional seeds. In his younger days, Jardhari was stirred by the Chipko Andolan, India's first environmental movement. Drawing inspiration from this, he set up an informal collective of farmers and activists to preserve local and traditional seed varieties, along with traditional agricultural practices. He received the **Indira Gandhi Environment Award** in 2009.

Green Action: Did you know that India has more than 200 types of rajma or kidney beans and more than 300 varieties of rice. Ask your grandparents about the variety of vegetables and lentils found in their time and if they are still found today. Start saving seeds and growing your own food in a pot!